THE TOUCH OF THE MASTER'S HAND

TO AMY, JOSIE,

AND DANIEL — GN

Special thanks to the Church of the Brethren Historical Library and Archives
and also all those who helped from Gold Leaf Press.
The poem appears as it did in 1936. Text Myra Brooks Welch.
Illustrations ©1996 Greg Newbold.
This is a Buckaroo Book, published by Gold Leaf Press.

Designed by Richard Erickson and Pat Bagley. Printed in Singapore by Tien Wah Press

10 9 8 7 6 5 4 3 2 1

Library of Congress Cataloging-in-Publication Data
Welch, Myra Brooks.
The touch of the master's hand / written by Myra Brooks Welch;
illustrated by Greg Newbold.
p.   cm.
ISBN 1-885628-03-X
1. Violin—Poetry.
I. Newbold, Greg (Gregory L.) II. Title.
PS3545.E515T6 1996
811' .52–dc20   96–11711
CIP

THE TOUCH OF THE MASTER'S HAND

WRITTEN BY MYRA BROOKS WELCH

ILLUSTRATED BY GREG NEWBOLD

Gold Leaf Press

'Twas battered and scarred, and the auctioneer
Thought it scarcely worth his while
To waste much time on the old violin,
But held it up with a smile:

What am I bidden, good folks," he cried,
"Who'll start the bidding for me?"
"A dollar, a dollar"; then, "Two!" "Only two?
Two dollars, and who'll make it three?

Three dollars, once; three dollars, twice;
Going for three–" But no,
From the room, far back, a gray-haired man
Came forward and picked up the bow;

Then, wiping the dust from the old violin,
And tightening the loose strings,

He played a melody pure and sweet
As a caroling angel sings.

The music ceased, and the auctioneer,
With a voice that was quiet and low,
Said: "What am I bid for the old violin?"
And he held it up with the bow.

A thousand dollars, and who'll make it two?
Two thousand! And who'll make it three?
Three thousand, once, three thousand, twice,
And going, and gone," said he.

The people cheered, but some of them cried,
"We don't quite understand
What changed its worth." Swift came the reply:

$$\text{T}\text{he touch of a master's hand.''}$$

And many a man with life out of tune,
And battered and scarred with sin,
Is auctioned cheap to the thoughtless crowd,
Much like the old violin.

A "mess of pottage," a glass of wine;

A game—and he travels on.

He is "going" once, and "going" twice,
He's "going" and almost "gone."

But the Master comes, and the foolish crowd
Never can quite understand
The worth of a soul and the change that's wrought
By the touch of the Master's hand.

Thought you would like this.

:-)

Forwarded message:

Date: Fri, 28 Jan 2000 13:47 -0600 (CST)
From: Michelle Davis <Michelle.Davis@mci.com>
Organization: MCI
To: Robb.Plemons@WCOM.COM,
    Maribel.Martinez-Cancino@WCOM.COM,
    Courtney.Williams@WCOM.COM,
    Joel.Jasenof@WCOM.COM,
    David.Rehm@WCOM.COM
Subject: FW: The Preacher's Wife

All,

Check this out!

An Illinois man left the snow-filled streets of Chicago for
a vacation in Florida. His wife was on a business trip and
was planning to meet him there the next day. When he
reached his hotel in Florida, he decided to send his wife a
quick e-mail. Unable to find the scrap of paper on which he
had written her e-mail address, he did his best to type it
in from memory.
Unfortunately, he missed one letter and his note was
directed instead to an elderly preacher's wife whose husband
had passed away only the day before. When the grieving
widow checked her e-mail, she took one look at the monitor,
let out a piercing scream and fell to the floor in a dead
faint.
At the sound, her family rushed into the room and saw this
note on the screen:

DEAREST WIFE: JUST GOT CHECKED IN.
EVERYTHING PREPARED FOR YOUR ARRIVAL TOMORROW.

PS.- SURE IS HOT DOWN HERE.